How do you like our book?

We would really appreciate you leaving us a review.

Other Picture Books:

For other fun Picture Books by Kampelstone,
simply search for:

Kampelstone Picture Books 🔍

FACTS ABOUT GREECE

- An old Greek legend says that when God created the world, he sifted all the soil onto the earth through a sieve. When all countries were completed with their good soil, God took the remaining stones that were left in the sieve and tossed them back over his shoulder, creating Greece.

- Greece has more international airports than most countries due to the huge influx of tourists each year.

- The population of Greece is close to eleven million people and about twelve million people around the world speak Greek.

- Greece has more than 2,000 islands but only about 170 are populated.

- Athens has been continuously inhabited for more than seven thousand years, making it the oldest city in Europe.

- Greece draws close to 17 million tourists each year, more than the country's total population.

- There are few retirement homes in Greece. Traditionally, Grandparents live with their children's family until they die. Also, most young people don't move away from their parents' home until they marry.

- In the 1950s, less than a third of the population could read and write. Now, literacy is greater than 95%.

- Many elements in Greek houses such as doors, windowsills, furniture, and church domes are painted a medium turquoise blue, especially in the Cyclades Islands. It is used because of an ancient belief that this shade of blue keeps evil away.

- The first Olympic Games were held in 776 BCE. The first Olympic champion was a Greek cook named Coroebus who won the sprint.

- Alexander the Great was the first Greek ruler to put his own face on coins. Before that, only gods and goddesses were on the Greek coins.

- There are some olive trees in Greece that were planted in the thirteenth century which are still producing olives.

- Greek has been spoken for more than 3,000 years, making it one of the oldest languages in Europe.

- forty percent of Greeks live in Athens.

- Greece's national anthem has 158 verses.

- Greece has more archaeological museums than any other country in the world.

- For centuries, the Greeks have been heavily involved in trade by ship all across the world. To this day, there are still numerous Greek shipping companies. Greek ships make up 70% of the European Union's total merchant fleet. According to Greek law, three fourths of a Greek ships' crew must be Greek.

- In Greece, voting is required by law for every citizen who is 18 or older. One cannot not vote.

- In Greece, people don't celebrate their birthday. Rather, they celebrate the "name day" of the saint for whom they were named.

- The saying "taking the bull by the horns" comes from the Greek myth of Hercules saving Crete from a raging bull by seizing its horns.

Printed in Poland
by Amazon Fulfillment
Poland Sp. z o.o., Wrocław
27 December 2022

9ef9ae51-0520-4ba8-9d9f-4fa13eff2601R01